Pretend You're a Grownup

Karen Bryant-Mole

Heinemann Interactive Library
Des Plaines, Illinois

Published by Heinemann Interactive Library,
an imprint of Reed Educational & Professional Publishing,
1350 East Touhy Avenue, Suite 240 West
Des Plaines, IL 60018

Produced by Times Offset (M) Sdn. Bhd.

Designed by Jean Wheeler

Commissioned photography by Zul Mukhida

02 01 00 99 98
10 9 8 7 6 5 4 3 2 1

Library of Congress Cataloging-in-Publication Data

Bryant-Mole, Karen.
    You're a grown-up/Karen Bryant-Mole.
       p. cm. -- (Pretend)
    Includes biographical references and index.
    Summary: Explains the different kinds of work which adults do
around the home and suggests ways to pretend to accomplish grown-up
tasks such as shopping, cooking, gardening, and washing the car.
    ISBN 1-57572-185-6
    1. Adulthood--Juvenile literature. 2. Home economics--Juvenile
literature (1. Adulthood. 2. Home ecomomics.) I. Title.
II. Series: Bryant-Mole, Karen. Pretend.
HQ799.95.B79 1997
305.24--dc21   97-16971
                                                        CIP
                                                        AC

Acknowledgments
The author and publishers are grateful to the following for permission to reproduce
copyright photographs:
Chapel Studios: 7 and 15 Zul Mukhida; Positive Images: 5; Tony Stone Images: 9 Lawrence Migdale,
13 Lawrence Monneret, 23 Dan Bosler; Zefa: 11, 17, 19, 21

Cover photograph Zul Mukhida

Every effort has been made to contact copyright holders of any material reproduced in this book. Any
omissions will be rectified in subsequent printings if notice is given to the publisher.

Words in bold, **like this**, are explained in the glossary on page 24.

Contents

Shopping

Joseph is pretending that
he has been shopping
for food.
He is carrying the
groceries home
in a basket.

This woman brought her groceries home
in the car.
A week's worth of groceries for a hungry
family is much too heavy to carry home.

Cooking

Asia is pretending to cook
some food.
She made her stove
from a cardboard box.

This man is cooking some soup.
Real stoves get very hot.
Never play with a real stove.

Mealtimes

Ethan is pretending to have a meal with his toys. They each have a knife, fork, and spoon.

These people are using chopsticks to eat their meal. They pick up their food by holding it between the two chopsticks.

9

Washing Dishes

Joseph is washing his toy tea set.
He has a plastic bowl, filled with warm, soapy water.

This woman uses
a dishwasher
to wash her
dishes.
She puts
everything in
and lets the
machine do all
the work.

Baby's Bedtime

Alysha is getting her doll
ready for bed.
She is pretending to wash
the doll's face.

This baby is having a bath before he goes to bed.
He doesn't look very sleepy yet!

Housework

Homes can get very dusty. Edward is using a toy broom to sweep the floor.

This woman is vacuuming her floor.
The dust is sucked up inside the machine.

Yard Work

Asia has a set of toy yard work tools. She is pretending to **rake** up leaves.

Yard work machines are very useful.
This man is using a lawn mower to
cut the grass.
It does the work quickly and easily.

Working

Melissa is pretending to work from home. She has set up an office with a play telephone and toy computer.

People who work from home use telephones, computers, and **fax machines** to keep in touch with other people.

Baking

William is using a small **rolling pin** to roll out some **play dough**. He will cut out some interesting shapes with plastic cookie cutters.

These children are helping to make
an apple pie.
The **dough** has been rolled and cut
out to fit into the pie dish.

21

Washing the Car

Melissa's toy car has gotten all muddy. She is using a damp cloth to clean it.

This boy is washing the car with a sponge.
His father is using clean water to rinse it.

Glossary

fax machines These machines can send and print words and pictures.

dough A mixture of flour, butter, and water that is used to make pie crusts is called dough.

play dough This is a clay-like mixture that can be rolled out, squashed, twisted, and squeezed.

rake This means to collect leaves or grass with a tool called a rake.

rolling pin This is a roller with a handle at each end.

Index

More Books to Read

Hudson, Wade. *I'm Gonna Be*. East Orange, NJ: Just US Books, 1992.

Kundstadter, Maria. *Women Working A to Z*. Fort Atkinson, WI: Highsmith Press, 1994.

Scarry, Richard. *What Do People Do All Day?* New York: Random House, 1968.